I0837737

WHO IS TO BLAME?

The Foundation of Challenges, Divisions, and Problems within the African Community in Australia

By Juma Abuyi

Table of Contents

Acknowledgments

I am grateful to the many great Australians who deal directly with people of African background (including friends) with whom I have worked over the years, and from whom I have learned so much. The knowledge I have shared in this booklet owes much to their involvement and contributions.

I thank my great friends Mabok Deng Marial, Dr Joseph Masika, Eugenia Tsoulis, Enaam Oudih, Kym and Fiona Foster, Coby and David Vautin, Vicky and Joe Jordan, and Lou and Matt Durose who have always been available to discuss any issues relating to the African and Australian community at large. Not to forget the African community leaders, elders and members whose practices and ideologies let me to research and write this booklet.

I acknowledged that you all have given me the opportunity to verify my thoughts and knowledge about Australia. Please know that you have given me the energy, emotional support and encouragement to write this book and to enjoy the privilege of resettlement in Australia.

Dr. Juma Abuyi
Adelaide 2020

Foreword

The question of who is to blame for African community issues in Australia presents challenges to the privileges available in the African resettlement process in Australia. It is expected that African Australians will enjoy the freedoms brought through the resettlement process, yet many have encountered worries, glitches and hitches with their peaceful settlement in this land of great opportunity. Confined within small prison cells, many youths and adults dream of the life they once had in refugee camps and in their countries of origin on the African continent. Australia, the land of opportunity, has become a monster that swallows African individuals, families and communities one by one. Who is to blame for these unfolding glitches? This Author attempts to analyse and understand the issues within the African community in Australia. While not all African communities experience the same kinds of challenges, difficulties and divisions, the Author presents some of the pressing issues endured by many African communities in Australia. Expecting solutions from outside the African community is the same as seeking to catch the wind by chasing it. It is time for the African and Australian community to wake up to the call for it to change as the answers to these problems lie within the African community itself.

The Foundation of Challenges, Divisions, and Problems within the African Community in Australia

Introduction

This booklet attempts to analyse and understand the issues within the African community in Australia. While not all African communities experience the same kinds of challenges, difficulties and divisions, the booklet presents some of the general issues endured by many African communities in Australia. The Author discusses the issues that bring divisions within the African community, such as the skilled stream versus the refugee group, the major regions of Africa, the concept of education, mainstream services and the implications of 'understanding' and 'misunderstanding'. The readers and affected African community groups, must find solutions to these problems. Expecting solutions from outside the African community is the same as seeking to catch the wind by chasing it. It is time for the African community to wake up to the call for it to change as the answers to their problems lie within the community itself.

Skilled stream versus refugee group

People of African background arriving in Australia are divided into several major categories using different criteria. Firstly, people are grouped according to how they entered Australia, whether through a 'migration program' (the skilled stream) or a 'humanitarian program' (the refugee group).[1] The individuals who enter Australia through the skilled migration stream may have some finances and some language skills, and they may find it much easier to gain employment than those in the refugee group. As a result, their general living standard may be much higher than those who came through the refugee/humanitarian channel, and they may choose to distance themselves from the so-called 'refugee group'. Those in the skilled migration group are also distanced from the refugee group by service providers, due to their funding agreements. Hence, by necessity, they form a unique group that serves its own interests. This develops a very large imagined gap between the skilled stream group and the refugee/humanitarian group. It also creates difficulties for people from the same background working together. Yet, for a small group of African communities in Australia, life is 'better together'.[2] This division exists but no one wants to talk about it. According to research conducted in the United States of America (USA), social scientists see migrant communities as culturally deprived, owing to this reinforced internal division within the African American communities.[3] In addition, a World Bank study carried out in 2014 states that division within the community created problems for policy development.[4]

Major rregions of Africa

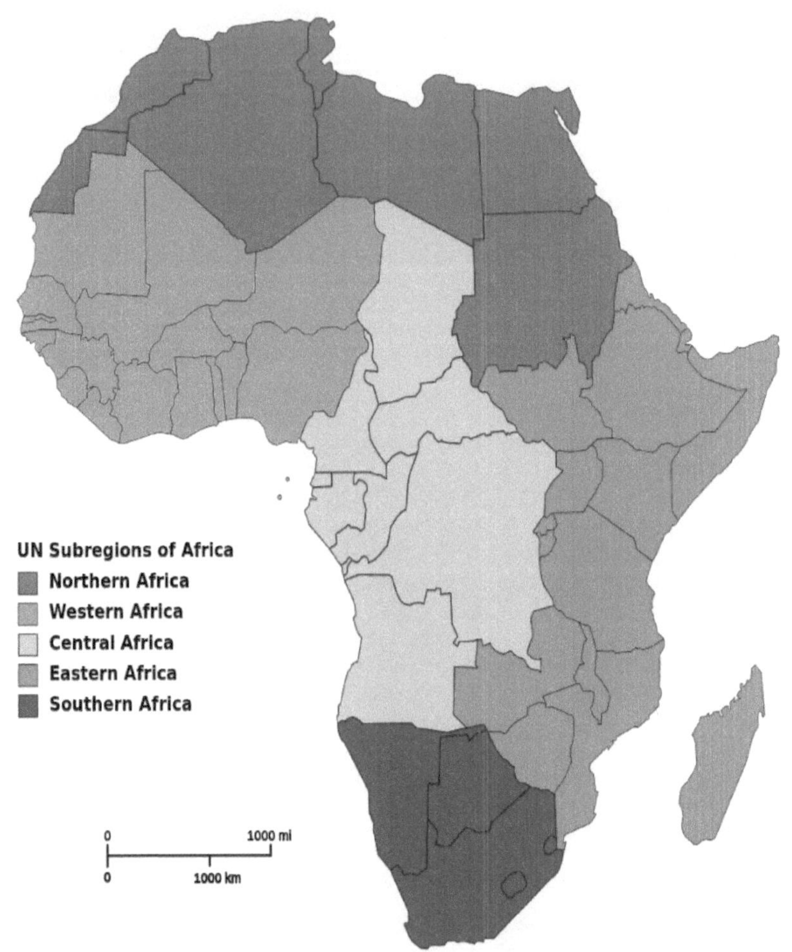

Secondly, people of African background in Australia are categorised based on the five major regions of Africa: southern Africa, eastern Africa, northern Africa, central Africa and western Africa.[5] However, northern Africa—which includes countries such as Sudan, Egypt, Libya, Morocco, Algeria and Tunisia—has been excluded from the sub-Saharan African group and combined with the Middle Eastern region.[6] It is true that northern Africa is largely Arabic, with historical, religious and cultural connections to the Middle East.[7] This historical creation is divisive, especially in Western societies, but also in Africa, as a greater population of Arabs lives on the African continent than in the Middle East. These divisions not only occur on paper but also when planning to offer services to these people in Western countries.

Service providers in Australia who receive government funding follow the same system of categorisation. A good example of these services is offered by the Middle Eastern Communities Council of South Australia Inc. (MECCSA) and the African Communities Council of South Australia Inc. (ACCSA) in South Australia. Similar services could also be offered in other Australian cities. This distribution of services divides the African community: as a result, people from one region tend to view their region as more important than other regions of Africa. The defining features of communication, socialisation and support remain within these boundaries of partition. These ideologies are not only destroying relationships between these groups and other African community groups but are also destroying their connection with the wider Australian society. These kinds of division have left the African continent in chaos[8] and African people in Australia cannot afford to think along the same lines. The same issues have been reported in the United States of America (USA).[9] African people need to think beyond their comfort zone to come up with something different: they should never expect different outcomes when thinking in the same way. In other words, African people in Australia should not expect change when they continue to follow structures that create more division in their community, instead of enriching unity in their own life and the lives of the people for whom they care. At least pardoned may exist for people of African background living in Africa but for those in Australian society, it is essential that they work together.

Concept of education

The third issue dividing people of African background in some African communities in Australia is their concept of 'education'. Education is meant to offer opportunities for individuals to develop 'skills and competencies in support of subsequent employment enabling people to become more constructive and active members of society'.[10] While the African community values education highly, the attitudes and actions of some of its members towards educated individuals are both discouraging and unpleasant. It may be surprising but for many community members, education is seen as grounds for differentiation. People of African background— particularly African community elders, both men and women, who were deprived of education or never took the opportunity in Australia to educate themselves—see educated individuals as opponents who are 'showing off'. It is also a possibility that those individuals who consider themselves educated may be showing off or failing to treat those with no education ethically. Of course, this can be painful, especially when those from the educated group represent the community in leadership positions, while the uneducated group in that community had no previous opportunities to educate themselves. These kinds of African community attitudes and behaviours limit the intellectual contribution to the African community. They also discourage African youth and some adults from taking education seriously, for fear of offending others and to show their support to the elders. As a result, divisions develop which contribute to the failure to thrive of the African community, its leadership and its human capital in Australia.

Mainstream services

The fourth issue dividing the African community in Australia is mainstream services, even though the provision of services to people of African background is an integral part of Australia's current endeavour to offer a practical and suitable environment for African people and other Australians at large. In the following subsections, this issue is broken down into two parts: firstly, the systematic approach to service provision and, secondly, service providers from within the African community supporting their own interests.

Systematic approach to service provision

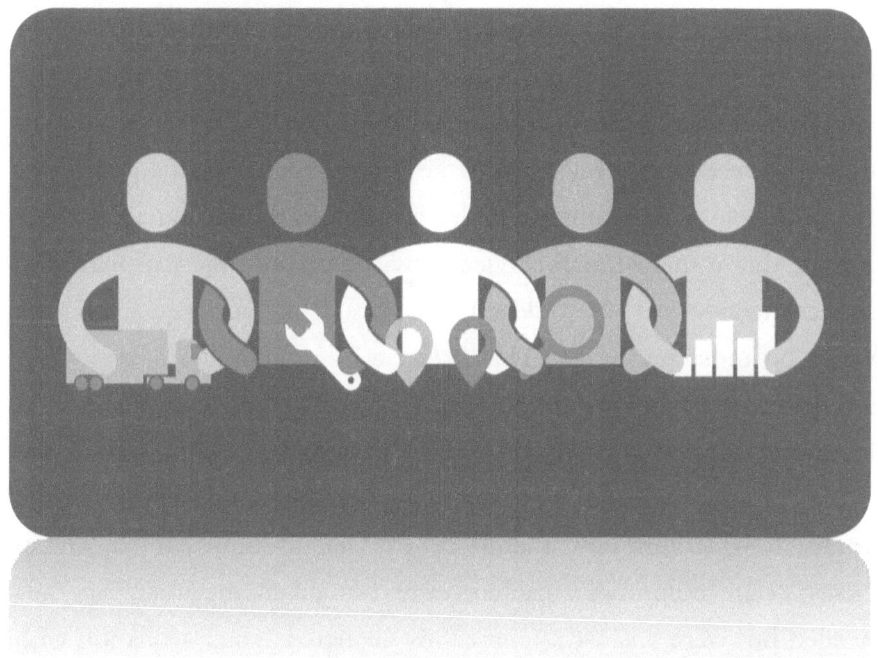

A systematic approach to service provision is the key to providing appropriate services, especially to refugees/migrants and humanitarian entrants to Australia. After working for many years within service provider agencies, the writer has noticed that some problems within the African community and its leadership have been initiated by mainstream service providers, especially those involved in delivering services to people of African or migrant background. This is not an accusation but an analysis of what the writer saw happening within the groups of migrants and refugees, including humanitarian entrants. As a researcher, the writer therefore sought to further investigate some of the problems within the leadership of African communities. The motivation for this work was to determine from where these leadership problems originated. In most cases, the interests of the African communities' leadership were divided in terms of receiving services from key mainstream service providers. For example, one community leader reported that he could not believe that a mainstream service provider responsible for providing services to new arrivals could refuse to grant him support at the time when he most needed it. This leader was undergoing a leadership struggle and was asking for financial support for his community and emotional support for himself. While this situation was unfolding, the other community leader was being supported and advised to win the attention of community members. In fact, at times of leadership crises, some community leaders were not given the attention they needed but were, instead, significantly alienated. Their affiliation with the mainstream service providers involved was reduced to zero. That leader may be left to suffer on his own while community members follow the leaders who are supported by service providers. This is a betrayal of the community.[11] Essamuah and Ngaruiya state that, in a situation like this, many community members fight for opposition and affiliation.[12] They struggle with multiple loyalties, yet it is a matter of sadness and shame when selfish gain is the motivation for the scuffle.

Supporting their own interests

When community leaders and the leadership of communities have problems amongst themselves, it is unfortunate that some service providers make no serious attempts to resolve the issues at hand. Instead, they support one leader and ignore the presence of the other. For example, in the process of writing this article, the writer had a conversation with one community leader. He narrated his experience with a service provider, in which he claimed that he was expelled from a building for what he considered unreasonable and inexplicable reasons. As a result, he felt abandoned, neglected and isolated. This experience is not new. In 2013, Essamuah and Ngaruiya[13] state that, in this kind of situation, the immigrants feel an undeniable foreignness. Unfortunately, this type of incident does not teach the leader a good lesson but serves only to confirm a preconceived assumption about that service provider. In the end, the above-mentioned leader came to believe that some of the issues within the African communities' leadership were linked to mainstream service providers.

At times, things happen without being noticed, especially when major issues strike the community. Many organisations working with people of African background rush to offer support, which is a good response, but no lead agency takes charge or asks the hard questions. After a short period, especially when things start to settle down, the community is left to carry its burden on its own. Hence, attention is needed to improve this area. The service providers have the great privilege of understanding the Australian system but, at times, if things are not done properly, it may appear that they are taking advantage of vulnerable African communities or turning one African community against the other. However, on the other side of the coin, the African community leadership has a responsibility. They should be vigilant and take steps to reflect on their activities with service providers, refraining from taking sides while, instead, focusing on creating partnerships with any organisation that is ready to provide services to people of African background in Australia. This viewpoint can be very challenging when, for example, the African community's leadership becomes attracted to service provider politics and refuses to associate with a government-funded organisation which could offer services to his community. As a result, community members lose services that were meant to aid their peaceful settlement in Australia.

Implications of 'understanding' and 'misunderstanding'

Finally, one of the most important issues dividing the African community in Australia comprises the concepts of 'understanding' and 'misunderstanding'. The issues of understanding and misunderstanding between the African community leadership and African communities, including service providers, is problematic and has many implications not only for African leaders but also for their community members and Australian society at large. According to LeBaron[14], everyone needs to absorb 'understanding' but much misinterpretation of understanding itself occurs. Understanding involves the expressive construction of argument. Basically, we must have certain standards, with these likely to change as we become more knowledgeable about accepting each other's lack of understanding.

The most important issue in the concepts of understanding and misunderstanding is the flow of communication. The African community leadership in Australia must grasp the need for clear communication in relation to the information given not only to African community members but also to any service provider. Service providers also must understand the possible influence of miscommunication. It could be that African community leaders may not understand service providers owing to a cultural misconception but that is not the only problem—English is a foreign language to these African community leaders, except for those born in Australia. The writer, in using his personal experience, states that in his minor leadership role within African community groups, he always found it difficult to recognise and understand the accents, concepts and ideas of some colleagues, service providers and stakeholders. Even though their words were spoken in English, the meaning may have been quite different, or his interpretation of the words may have been confused. In addition, it is possible that service providers would have blamed him for misinterpretation of, and misunderstanding, their information, even though some were not offering adequate or essential details and he had to fill in the missing links. It is thus important that service providers make a special effort to explain everything very clearly, repeating certain important details several times, if necessary, with an interpreter. The same applies to African community leaders: they must always be prepared to repeat certain important points in their dealings with service providers, until they are satisfied that their messages have been successfully conveyed. No shame should be present when needing to repeat important information to their stakeholders. This repetition could be a time-consuming, shameful and expensive practice but it is essential when offering appropriate services to those who lead people of African background in Australia.

Conclusion

People of African background who have resettled in Australia are currently experiencing a range of problems; however, in this article, the writer only identifies problems relating to African community leadership. The reason is that leaders are believed to be one of the most critical elements in the successful functioning of community groups[15] and 'their organisation capabilities and ability to propose new initiatives that eventually are embraced by the entire community and transformed into community self-help projects are essential elements for promoting ... development'.[16]

In general, the common goal of serving the interests of African people in Australia has been divided in many ways, leading many African community organisations to become dysfunctional. These organisations were established to serve people of African background in Australia, but most remain dysfunctional and embroiled in leadership struggles, which the writer assumes to stem from division within the African community. The 'we-feeling' has never been achieved, even within the smallest sub-community.[17] In view of this, many young people are left without guidance or with fewer activities with which to occupy themselves. This may be the reason why some African youth have been led into criminal activities and general anti-social behaviours, or are experiencing health problems.

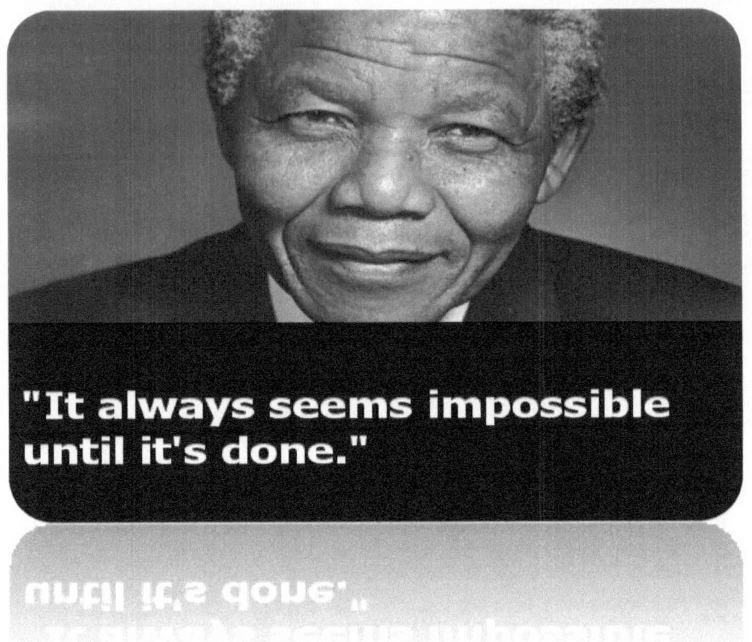

"What counts in life is not the mere fact that we have lived. It is what difference we have made to the lives of others that will determine the significance of the life we lead."

"Lead from the back -- and let others believe they are in front."

"As we let our own light shine, we unconsciously give other people permission to do the same."

Nelson Mandela

References

A World Bank Study. (2014). *Building Integrated Markets within the East Africa Community: EAC Opportunities in Public-Private Partnership Approaches to the Region's Infrastructure Needs.* Washington: The World Bank.

Ager, A. & Strang, A. (2008). Understanding Integration: A Conceptual Framework, *Journal of Refugees Studies*, 21 (2) pp.166-191.

Australian Bureau of Statistics (ABS) (2008) '*3416.0 - Perspectives on Migrants, 2008*', ABS, Canberra: ABS.

Davis, J. F. (1991). *Who is Black: One Nation's Definition.* University Park, Pennsylvania: Pennsylvania State University Press.

DIAC (2007) *Settlement Target Group Arrivals: July – December 2006,* Canberra: Commonwealth of Australia.

DIAC (2009) 'Fact Sheet 2- Key Facts in Immigration' *DIAC Media* URL: http://www.immi.gov.au/media/fact-sheets/02key.htm.

Essamuah, C. B. & Ngaruiya, D. K. (2013). *Communities of Faith in Africa and the African Diaspora: In Honor of Dr. Tite Tienou.* Eugene, Oregon: Pickwick Publications.

Kaplan, A (1996) *The Development Practitioners' Handbook,* London UK and Chicago, IL: Pluto Press

LeBaron, G. (2008). Captive Labour and the Free Market: Prisoners and Production in the USA. *Capital and Class,* 95 (Summer): 59–81.

Mbaku, J. M. (2007) *Corruption in Africa: Causes, Consequences, and Cleanups.* Lanham, MD: Lexington Books.

Mocombe, P. (2014). *Race and Class Distinctives within Black Communities: A Racial-Caste-In-Class.* New York: Routledge.

Murch, D. J. (2010). *Living for the City: Migration, Education, and the Rise of the Black Panther Party in Oakland, California.* North Carolina: The University of North Carolina Press.

Mwakikagile, G. (2006). *Tanzania Under Mwalimu Nyerere: Reflections on an African Statesman*, 2nd (Ed.) Dar es Salaam-Tanzania: New Africa Press.

Opare, S (2007) 'Strengthening Community-Based Organizations for the Challenges of Rural Development', *Community Development Journal* Vol. 42 No.2 251-264

Page, P. (1999). *Reclaiming Community in Contemporary African American Fiction.* Mississippi: University Press of Mississippi.

Putnam, D. R & Feldstein M. L (2003) *Better Together: Restoring the American Community*, New York: Don Cohen, Simon & Schuster, by Mowbray, M (2005) Reviews, Charles Darwin University, Darwin, Australia; Australia; martin.mobray@rmt.edu.au.

Rotberg, R. I. (2004). *State Failure and State Weakness in a Time of Terror*, Cambridge: World Peace Foundation.

Russell, K., Wilson, M. & Hall, R. (1992). *The Color Complex: The Politics of Skin Color among African Americans.* New York: Ancor.

Spencer, R. (1999). *Spurious Issues: Race and Multicultural Politics in the United States.* Boulder, CO: Westview Press.

Weisenfeld, J. & Newman, R. (1996). *This far by Faith: Reading in the African-American Women's Religious Biography.* London: Routledge.

22

ABOUT THE AUTHOR

Dr Juma Abuyi is a sociologist and social scientist involving in many different activities. His careers include community and sport development work, guest lecturing cultural studies, human resource management and research in particular with new and emerging multicultural communities. Dr Abuyi has served both federal and State governments for many years providing advice on the development of policy and programs for new arrivals and humanitarian entrants groups in Australia. Dr Abuyi has won several awards, including the South Australian Governor's Multicultural Award, South Australia Police Academic Award and the Champion Award for exceptional achievements and remarkable contributions to Australia and Africa through policing, social and community engagements. In 2014, he was awarded the Doctor of Human Service Research at the University of South Australia

---

[1] Department of Immigration and Citizenship (DIAC), 2007.
[2] Putnam & Feldstein, 2003.
[3] Murch, 2010.
[4] World Bank, 2014.
[5] Australian Bureau of Statistics (ABS), 2008.
[6] DIAC, 2009.
[7] Mwakikagile, 2006, p. 9.
[8] Rotberg, 2004; Mwakikagile, 2006; Mbaku, 2007.
[9] Spencer, 1999; Davis, 1991; Russell, Wilson and Hall, 1992; Mocombe, 2014; Page, 1999.
[10] Ager & Strang, 2008, p. 172.
[11] Weisenfeld & Newman, 1996.
[12] Essamuah & Ngaruiya, 2013.
[13] Essamuah & Ngaruiya, 2013.
[14] LeBaron, 2008.
[15] Kaplan, 1996.
[16] Opare, 2007, p. 257.
[17] Opare, 2007.

EndNote

www.ingramcontent.com/pod-product-compliance
Lightning Source LLC
Chambersburg PA
CBHW031922270726
48655CB00007BA/3258